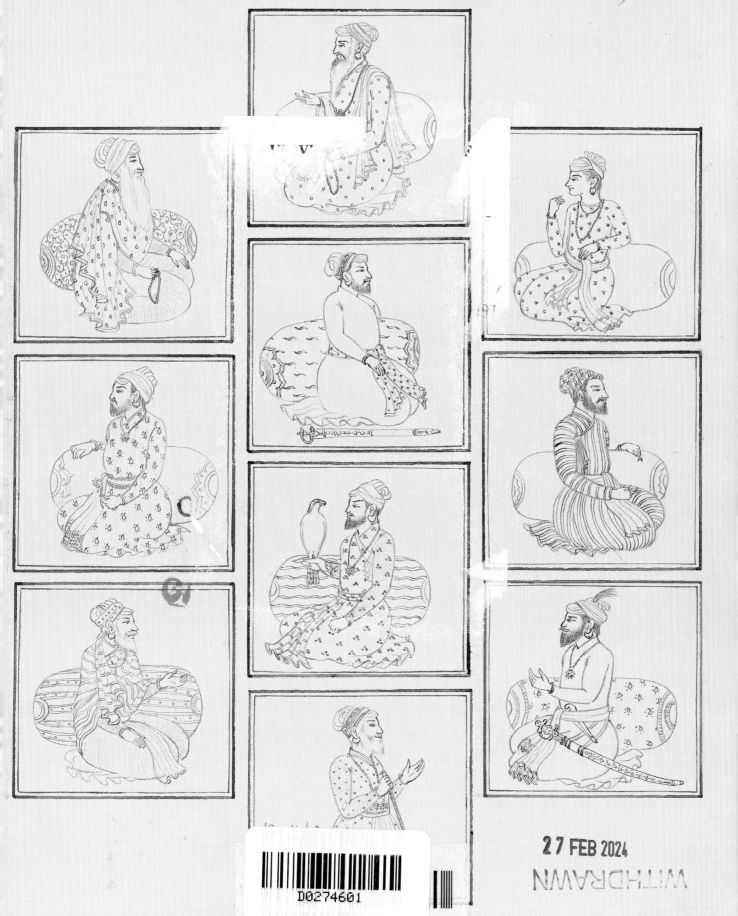

STORIES FROM
THE
SIKH
WORLD

written by

Rani and Jugnu Singh

illustrated by

Jeroo Roy

Macdonald

Managing Editor : Belinda Hollyer
Book Editor : Barbara Tombs
Design Concept : Liz Black
Production Controller : Rosemary Bishop

Consultant : Dr Owen Cole

A MACDONALD BOOK

© text Rani and Jugnu Singh 1987
© illustrations Macdonald & Co (Publishers) Ltd 1987

First published in Great Britain in 1987 by
Macdonald & Co (Publishers) Ltd
London & Sydney
A BPCC plc company

Printed in Great Britain by
Purnell Book Production Ltd
Member of the BPCC Group

Macdonald & Co (Publishers) Ltd
Greater London House
Hampstead Road
London NW1 7QX

British Library Cataloguing in Publication Data
Singh, Rani
   Stories from the Sikh world
   1. Sikhism—Juvenile literature
   I. Title   II. Singh, Jugnu
   294.6   BL2018

ISBN 0-356-13165-3

CONTENTS

The Wealthy Banker of Lahore

Guru Nanak was the first Guru. He spent much of his life travelling and teaching. During his travels he visited the city of Lahore, in what is now known as Pakistan. This is a very famous story of his meeting with one of the city's rich bankers.

Once, long ago, there lived a banker in the city of Lahore. His name was Duni Chand, and he was well known throughout the city for his greed and dishonesty. He lived in a beautiful palace, which shone with gold, marble and precious jewels.

One day, Duni Chand learnt that Guru Nanak had arrived in the city. At once Duni Chand rushed to find the Guru, so that he could invite him to a special feast in the Guru's honour. Guru Nanak accepted the invitation and preparations for the feast began.

It was a splendid occasion. Tasty dishes were set before the guests and in the background minstrels played soft music. The guests all agreed that it was a magnificent feast. When everyone had finished, Duni Chand turned to Guru Nanak. 'I am a wealthy man,' he said. 'If I can do anything for you, please tell me.'

Guru Nanak sat for a moment, deep in thought. He looked around at the splendour of the palace, the rich tapestries hanging on the wall and the fine golden dishes. Then, fumbling in his pocket, he drew out a slim case which contained a tiny, fine needle.

'Yes, there is something I would like you to do for me,' he replied, holding up the needle. 'I would like you to keep this needle very safely and give it back when we meet in the next world.' And with these words, the Guru left the feast.

Duni Chand felt full of importance. The Guru had entrusted him with such a special task. He took the needle and showed it to his wife, explaining what the Guru had told him. To his utter astonishment, she burst into peals of laughter.

'Oh, my poor husband,' she laughed. 'I should go back and ask Guru Nanak how you can take it to heaven with you.'

Feeling rather confused, Duni Chand hurried after the Guru, who was just disappearing around the corner of the street. 'Guru Nanak, Guru Nanak,' he called. 'Please tell me one thing before you go. How can I take this needle with me when I die?'

The Guru looked at Duni Chand kindly and said, 'If you cannot take a tiny needle with you when you die, how are you going to take all your riches? You will only be remembered for the good things you have done in this world when you go to the next.'

Duni Chand thought and realized the truth in the Guru's words. He felt ashamed of his actions and from that day on, he and his wife used their wealth to help the poor.

The Bowl of Milk and the Jasmine Flower

Guru Nanak was often accompanied on his travels by a faithful musician called Mardana, who was very fond of eating and drinking. One day, after a long and tiring journey, they approached the city of Multan.

Mardana was hot and tired and dusty. He and Guru Nanak had been travelling for many days and nights, with little to eat and drink. He longed to get to Multan, where there was a chance of a good meal and a welcome rest. Slowly, he trudged alongside Guru Nanak towards the distant city.

Now the city of Multan was famous because many priests and holy men lived there. People came from far and wide to ask their help and advice and gave them presents or money in return. The priests and holy men had grown rich and comfortable and certainly didn't want any more of their kind in the city. When they heard that Guru Nanak and Mardana were nearing the city gates, they all met together to plan what to do.

They decided that a messenger should carry a bowl full of milk to Guru Nanak. It was to be so full that there wasn't room for a single drop more. By giving this to the Guru, the priests wanted him to know that there were already plenty of priests and holy men in the city and there was no room for any more.

The messenger took the bowl. Slowly and carefully he walked, his eyes fixed on the milk. Slowly and carefully, one foot in front of the other, until he reached Guru Nanak and Mardana. He handed the bowl to Guru Nanak.

Mardana looked longingly at the bowl of milk and then looked at Guru Nanak. He was so thirsty; how he wished the Guru would accept it so that he could drink. But the Guru didn't reach out to take the bowl. Instead, he bent down and plucked a beautiful jasmine flower which was growing nearby. Saying nothing, he dropped the flower into the bowl. It floated delicately, scenting the milk. Not a drop of milk had been spilt.

'Take this message to the priests and holy men of Multan,' the Guru said to the messenger. 'Tell them that just as there was room for the jasmine flower to scent a bowlful of milk, so there is always room for holiness and goodness in this world.'

Hearing the Guru's message, the priests and holy men felt ashamed of their behaviour. They apologized for their rudeness and came to welcome Guru Nanak and Mardana to their city.

The Jealous Brother

The fourth guru, Guru Ram Das, had three sons. The eldest was Prithia, the second was Mahan Dev, and the youngest was Arjan. Of the three, Arjan was the Guru's favourite. He was hardworking and spent much of his time in prayer. Prithia was very jealous of his youngest brother. He thought his father would make Arjan the next Guru. One day the Guru sent Arjan to the city of Lahore.

Arjan was sad and lonely. He was far from home and he missed his family and friends terribly. Had the brook at the bottom of the garden run dry in the summer heat? Who was looking after his beloved goats while he was away? He hadn't heard from his father for a long, long time.

'I know what I'll do,' he said to himself one day, 'I'll send him a message in a poem.'

He looked around him and saw a bird sitting just above his head, looking down at him from a mango tree. Then he wrote on a piece of paper:

'As the Chatrik bird cries for raindrops,
So do I long for you, oh Father!'

He folded the letter and sent it to his father in Amritsar. But Prithia had been expecting a message from Arjan. When he saw the letter, he managed to get hold of it first and hide it away. He sent a note back to Arjan, pretending it was from his father, telling him to stay on in Lahore a little longer.

Days passed; weeks passed. No further news came to Arjan. 'Has my father forgotten me?' he said quietly to himself. He sent another verse of his poem.

'I pine for you as a Sarang bird
Who pines for water, oh father.'

Again he sent the message to Amritsar. But his wicked brother was watching out for it. Again he hid the message away.

Arjan grew worried, 'I wonder what is wrong? Why haven't I heard from my father?' He took another sheet of paper, carefully wrote the number three on it and gave it to a messenger, telling him to give it to no one but his father, Guru Ram Das.

The Guru guessed that the number three meant two letters had been sent before. He called Prithia.

'What is the meaning of this?' he asked, showing Prithia the letter. 'I haven't received any other letters apart from this one. Do you know what has happened to the other two?'

Prithia stood silently, looking down at his feet.

'I don't know what you mean,' he said at last.

The Guru didn't reply. Instead he sent two men to search Prithia's belongings. There they found the two letters from Arjan. They brought them to the Guru, who held them in front of Prithia.

'But Father,' Prithia stuttered. 'I wrote those myself.'

The Guru knew how to find out the truth. He sent a message for Arjan to return to Amritsar. When Arjan finally arrived before the Guru, tired after his long journey, but happy to be home, the Guru said to both his sons, 'Say the next verse of the poem.'

Prithia couldn't think of anything at all and stood speechless. But Arjan immediately said,

'By good luck I have found the saint,
Indeed I have found good luck in my house.'

Guru Ram Das was delighted with Arjan and said that he deserved to be the next Guru for he had behaved well and honestly.

Prithia became red with anger. 'B-B-But I am your eldest son!' he spluttered. 'I deserve all that you have. What do I get?'

Arjan spoke quietly:

'Father, please give Prithia all the land and the house and everything you own. I need neither house nor money. God will give me all I need.'

'Very well,' said Guru Ram Das, 'Prithia, you will take everything I own. And you Arjan, will become Guru after me.'

And so it happened. Arjan became the fifth leader of the Sikhs, a wise and good Guru. But Prithia never overcame his jealousy. For many years he remained Guru Arjan's enemy.

The Princes and the Guru's Cloak

The Emperor Jahangir had a special friendship with Guru Har Gobind. It was a friendship which many of the Emperor's ministers and officials looked on with mistrust, particularly one official named Chandu. When the Emperor fell ill, Chandu saw his chance of sending the Guru away from the palace.

The Emperor was very sick. He was becoming weaker and weaker by the day. 'Bring me my wise men, Chandu,' he asked. 'I will ask them what to do to get rid of this illness.'

So Chandu fetched the wise men. But before he led them in to see the Emperor, he took them to one side. He told them why the Emperor had called for them. Then he offered the wise men a huge reward if they promised to tell the Emperor exactly what Chandu told them to say. Now the sum of money Chandu named was extremely large and the wise men were extremely greedy. They happily agreed to do as Chandu asked.

Then Chandu took the wise men in to see the Emperor and they stood before him in the hushed, darkened room. 'What must I do to rid myself of this illness?' the Emperor asked quietly.

The wise men bowed politely before replying. 'Emperor, you must send a holy man of God to the fort of Gwalior. There he must pray for your recovery,' they said, just as Chandu had told them.

'Then you must send Guru Har Gobind,' Chandu added quickly. 'No one is holier than he is.'

And so the Emperor agreed, and Guru Har Gobind was sent to Gwalior. The Guru was certain that it was part of a plot against him, but there was nothing he could do about it.

When Guru Har Gobind arrived at the fort, he found there fifty-two princes, or rajas, who were being held prisoner. They were very dejected. They had little food, their clothes were dirty and they were treated very badly.

The Guru felt very sorry for them. He shared his food with them and managed to get them clean clothes. His good humour cheered them up enormously and the prisoners were glad of his company.

Many months later, when the Emperor had at last recovered, he called Guru Har Gobind back to his palace. The prisoners were sad when they heard that the Guru was leaving them. 'Don't worry,' he assured them. 'I won't leave unless you can all come too.'

Guru Har Gobind sent a message to the Emperor that he would stay at the fort unless the other prisoners were freed with him. 'But I couldn't possibly free them all,' thought the Emperor. He sent a message back to the Guru, saying that the Guru could take as many of those who could hold on to his cloak as he came through the gateway of the fort.

The gateway was very narrow, so the Guru knew he would have to think of a clever plan if he was to get all the princes out with him. He had a special cloak brought to him, with fifty-two silken tassels. He gathered the princes around him and told them of his plan. Not one would be left behind!

Sure enough, when the gates were opened, not five, not ten princes followed the Guru out of the fort, holding on to his cloak. All fifty-two pushed and jostled their way through the narrow gateway, each clutching tightly on to a silk tassel.

Guru Har Gobind's plan had worked. Because of this he came to be known as Bandi Chhorr – the holy man who freed prisoners.

The Merchant and the Five Hundred Gold Coins

At one time, there were many people who lived in Bakala, a small village near Amritsar, who claimed to be the true Guru. This story tells of how a merchant called Makhan Shah discovered who the true Guru really was.

It was a stormy night. The wind howled and shrieked and lightning lit up the sky. A small boat tossed about helplessly on the angry sea. At times it was almost hidden by the huge waves. Makhan Shah, the owner, peered out anxiously at the storm-filled sky.

Makhan Shah was a merchant. He had been sailing with all his goods of silks and fine perfumes along the west coast of India, when the storm had blown up. Now it seemed almost certain that both he and his ship would be lost.

Makhan Shah closed his eyes. He folded his hands together and prayed over and over again. 'Dear God, please, please save my ship. I will give five hundred gold coins in thanks to you, if you help us to reach the shore safely.'

When Makhan Shah opened his eyes, he was astounded to see land looming ahead. How relieved he was as he carefully guided his ship towards the shore. His prayers had been answered; he and his ship had been saved.

Remembering his promise, Makhan Shah set out immediately to make the long journey to the village of Bakala where he had heard the Guru lived, so that he could offer him the gold coins. But he hadn't expected to find quite so many gurus in Bakala. They all claimed to be the true Guru, but how could he know which one to believe? Which guru should he give the five hundred gold coins to?

He thought for a while and then decided on his plan. 'I will visit each guru in turn and offer him just two gold coins. The false gurus will take the money. Only the true Guru will know how much I really promised to pay. That way I will know who the real Guru is.'

And that is what he did. He entered the first house, where a man sat cross-legged on a grand throne. He placed the two gold coins in front of him.

'Welcome my son. How generous and how clever you are to have come to the one true Guru,' he said. 'And what a fine jacket you have,' he added, eyeing the gold embroidery on Makhan Shah's jacket. Makhan Shah left the house quickly. This certainly wasn't the true Guru.

One by one Makhan Shah visited each of the so-called gurus. Each time the same thing happened. They all said they were the true Guru and took the two gold coins, but not one had seemed surprised that Makhan Shah hadn't given the rest of the money he had promised.

Makhan Shah began to despair. He so wanted to keep his promise. Finally, he asked an old man if there were any other gurus living in the village. The old man tugged at his beard before replying. 'Well,' he said, 'there is a quiet man called Tegh Bahadur who lives on the outskirts of the village. He keeps himself to himself and hardly ever comes out to meet anyone. He seems to spend most of his days praying. Perhaps he's the Guru you are looking for.'

Makhan Shah thanked the old man and hurried off. There in a small hut on the outskirts of the village he found Tegh Bahadur praying quietly. Makhan Shah placed the two gold coins in front of him.

Tegh Bahadur opened his eyes slowly. He looked at the two gold coins and then he looked at Makhan Shah.

'But what is this?' he asked Makhan Shah. 'You are breaking your promise. When your ship was sinking you promised five hundred gold coins. Now you are offering only two. Why?'

Makhan Shah's face lit up with delight. 'At last!' he cried, 'I've found the true Guru.' He placed the five hundred gold coins at the Guru's feet and hugged him joyfully. Then he rushed out to tell the news to the rest of the village. That night there was great rejoicing amongst the Sikhs. At last their true leader had been found.

The Story of Baisakhi

Baisakhi Day is celebrated in many parts of India, but for Sikhs it is an especially important festival. This story tells why.

It was springtime and Guru Gobind Singh had called his followers together for the festival of Baisakhi. The scent of spring flowers filled the air as his followers hurried up the hilltop to the fortress castle of Anandpur. There, a large tent had been set up. There was an excited hubbub as the people gathered around.

Suddenly the crowd fell silent as Guru Gobind Singh strode out on to the stage in front of the tent, an unsheathed sword in his hand. Everyone waited expectantly.

'Is there anyone among you who would lay down his life for God and his Guru?' he cried, looking at the crowd below him.

There was a shocked pause; no one spoke.

'Is there anyone among you who would lay down his life for God and his Guru?' his voice rang out, more loudly this time.

The people in the crowd turned to each other in disbelief. 'Has he called us here to die?' they asked one another. 'Surely he isn't serious.'

The Guru waited, imposingly. Then one man moved forward out of the crowd. His name was Daya Ram. 'I would willingly lay down my life for my God and my Guru,' he said steadily, looking at the Guru.

'Come with me,' replied the Guru and led him into the tent. The people watching held their breath. Suddenly there was a whoosh, then a thud. Guru Gobind Singh returned to the crowd, holding his sword in the air. It seemed to be dripping with blood. They all watched, stunned.

'Who will be next?' he cried. 'Who else will lay down his life for God and his Guru?'

The people were horrified. Why was their Guru doing this?

'I will willingly lay down my life for God and my Guru,' came a second voice from the crowd. Another man stepped forward.

The Guru led him into the tent. Again they heard a whoosh, followed by a thud. Once more the Guru reappeared with his sword apparently dripping with blood.

But the horror had not finished. Three times more the Guru asked the people his terrible question. Each time another volunteer came forward. The Guru disappeared into the tent with him and then returned to the crowd alone. Each time the crowd heard the terrible noise and saw what looked like a bloodstained sword. It was too much. The people watching were so shocked that many started running away in fear, sobbing.

Suddenly the Guru's voice could be heard above the terrified cries. 'Wait!' he called. 'Don't go! I have something to show you.' The people stopped and some started turning back. The Guru disappeared into the tent. A few minutes later he returned leading all five men, their hair neatly tied in turbans. The crowd gasped in disbelief. How could these men be alive? The Guru spoke:

'You all had so little faith, except for these five men. They alone have shown a very special kind of bravery. I will call these men the blessed five.'

The Guru pointed to the men standing next to him:

'I want all Sikhs to be brave and fearless like they were. We will form a brotherhood called the Khalsa. Everyone will be equal and we will all share the same name. Sikh men will be called Singh (which means lion) and Sikh women will be called Kaur (which means princess).

'So that people know we are Sikhs, we will wear special signs. We will wear our hair uncut, tied up and kept in place with a small comb and covered by a turban. On our wrists we will wear a steel bangle, because steel stands for strength and courage. We will carry a sword to protect the weak and ourselves. So that we can ride our horses with ease, we will wear special trousers. We will learn to live, work and play together as equals. With our special appearance we cannot hide anywhere in the world. We will always be noticed for what we do.'

Then the Guru blessed the men. He took a bowl of sweetened holy water called amrit and stirred it with a small sword. He gave the five some of this water to drink and then sprinkled it over their heads. As he did so he made them members of the new family, the Khalsa. It is said that at the end of the day over 20,000 people became members in this way.

The Donkey and the Tiger Skin

After the first amrit ceremony, at the festival of Baisakhi, Guru Gobind Singh wanted to encourage his followers to be brave and wear the special Khalsa uniform.

Once, long ago, Guru Gobind Singh was riding through the city of Anandpur when he heard a donkey braying in pain. In the distance he saw the potter's donkey, struggling under a heavy load. Passers-by were laughing and making fun of the poor helpless beast. The Guru felt sorry for the donkey. He thought how differently the donkey would have been treated had it been a tiger. As he continued on his way, an idea began to take shape in his mind.

When he arrived home the Guru looked for the tiger skin that had once been given to him as a gift by another Sikh. When he had found it, he sent some of his friends to rescue the potter's donkey. They brought him to the Guru who placed the tiger skin over the unsuspecting donkey's back. The Guru led the donkey back towards the village and let him go.

As the donkey walked into the village market place, he was astonished to see the goats and sheep jumping out of his way in fear. To his amazement, women and children screamed in terror and ran away. Market stall holders saw him coming and fled. He heard people shouting, 'Help! Help! A tiger!' Suddenly the market was quite deserted.

For the first time in a long while, the potter's donkey began to enjoy himself. He helped himself to the ripest fruit from the market stalls. He feasted on his favourite vegetables. When he had eaten his fill, he went in search of his master, the potter. But when he saw a tiger approach him, the potter too fled from his wheel in panic.

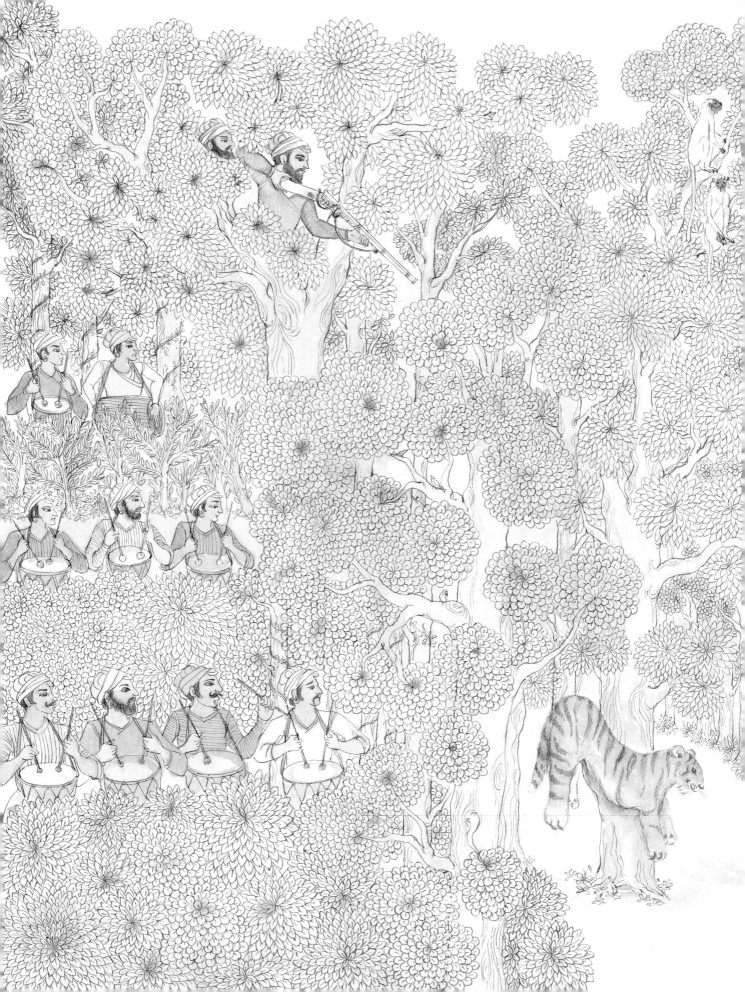

Quickly the villagers met together to decide what to do. They had to rid the village of the tiger. 'I think we should beat the hunting drums,' said an elderly man. 'Only then can we frighten the tiger back into the jungle.' And so it was decided that they should ask the Guru to form a hunting party.

With a loud beating of drums, the hunting party chased the bewildered animal into the forest. The poor donkey was terrified. He started to bray in panic, 'Hee haw! Hee haw!' Everyone stood stock still. What an extraordinary noise for a tiger to make! As the donkey turned round and round in circles, braying wildly, the tiger skin caught on a nearby tree and the skin slipped to the ground.

'Well! If it isn't the potter's donkey!' exclaimed one of the villagers. There were great roars of laughter and deep sighs of relief as all the villagers realized what had happened.

The Guru rubbed the donkey's nose gently and then said, 'Remember what happened to the potter's donkey. He wore the skin of a tiger, but his actions were still those of a donkey. In the same way you now wear the special Khalsa uniform. Make sure that your actions are brave and noble too.'

The Water-carrier

Guru Gobind Singh's men had been fighting against Emperor Aurangzeb's troops for many weeks. The Sikh fortress was surrounded and they were under siege. Many soldiers had been wounded and killed on both sides, yet still the bitter fighting continued.

The hot sun burnt down relentlessly on the dusty plain. In the distance a man could be seen, picking his way through the wounded and dying. He was carrying a bag of water. Every so often he bent down to give water to one of the soldiers.

A group of weary Sikh soldiers were watching him as he moved among the men. They recognized that he was a Sikh called Bhai Ghanaya. As they watched him more closely, they noticed that he was also giving water to the enemy soldiers as well as their own. They hurried to find the Guru and complained bitterly.

'Are we supposed to be fighting the enemy or not?' they muttered angrily. 'Bhai Ghanaya is giving water to everyone, friend and foe alike.'

The Guru sent for Bhai Ghanaya. 'Is it true that you have been giving water to the enemy?' he asked.

'When I walked through the battlefield I only saw the wounded. Some are badly injured and will surely die. It was the least I could do to give them water, whether they are friends or enemies,' Bhai Ghanaya replied.

Guru Gobind Singh smiled. 'I am pleased with you,' he said. 'We should always help those in need, whoever they may be.'

Bhai Ghanaya turned to go. 'Wait! Take this ointment,' added the Guru. 'When you give water to the wounded, put some of this ointment on their wounds too. Then you will be acting like a true Sikh of mine.'

The Sikh and the Buddhist

In March 1959, the peacefulness of the quiet mountains of Tibet was shattered. China had invaded Tibet and the religious leader of the Tibetan people, the Dalai Lama, was fleeing for his life.

Harmander Singh looked out from the village of Bomdila, over the mountains towards the border with Tibet. He had just received word from the Indian government that he was to meet the Dalai Lama and bring him to safety. But there were four different routes over the border. He did not know which one the Dalai Lama would take. He had to try and find out quickly.

Harmander Singh studied maps and spoke to the people who lived in the area. He decided that the route the Dalai Lama was most likely to choose was one bringing him to the border near a place called Tawang, where there was a large Buddhist monastery.

Harmander set off with a party of twenty-six Assam riflemen. The journey was hard. The route was full of dense thicket. Men were sent on ahead to clear a way through the undergrowth so the rest of the party could follow on easily. They travelled without stopping, not even to sleep, and ate berries and fruit from the forest. They rode fast, for they had an important mission.

Finally they heard that the Dalai Lama had arrived at the border. They found him in the midst of a large gathering of people, who were quietly unpacking their ponies and walking around, looking anxiously about them, fearful of attack.

Harmander Singh dismounted and went up to the Dalai Lama. He saw before him a young man, looking tired, but cheerful. It is a custom amongst Buddhists to exchange scarves on meeting each other, so Harmander Singh carried a long, white silk scarf. The Dalai Lama also had one. Harmander Singh bowed and offered him the scarf, welcoming him to India. The Dalai Lama took it, thanking him, and offered Harmander his scarf in return.

As the Dalai Lama's journey had been very hard, they rested for two days before continuing their journey to the monastery at Tawang, and then on through the narrow mountain passes to Bomdila. Harmander Singh rode close to the Dalai Lama all the way, to protect him against attack by the enemy. At night, he watched over the Dalai Lama whilst he slept. Throughout the journey, followers of the Dalai Lama who lived in this border region heard that he and his party were coming and they left their homes to watch them pass. There was a joyful atmosphere, as some people threw flower petals in their path, whilst others played music and blew trumpets loudly. They burnt incense and offered the travellers food and drink. It was a very special moment for them to have seen their leader.

Harmander Singh finally brought the party to safety in Bomdila. Shortly after many thousands of Buddhist refugees fled from Tibet, following the Dalai Lama. Many were injured on their journey. Harmander Singh took care of these people and gave them safety in India. For his courage and bravery he was later given an important award called the Padma Shri, by the Indian Government.

Background Notes

The Wealthy Banker of Lahore

This story has been taken from the 'Janam Sakhis' – a collection of stories about Guru Nanak's life (1469–1539 CE). These describe Guru Nanak's journeys to many parts of the Punjab as well as places outside India such as Baghdad, Makkah, Tibet and Sri Lanka. They illustrate many of the Guru's teachings. A few of the most important principles that Guru Nanak taught were to help the needy and live an honest and sincere life. He also championed the cause of women, treating them as equals. He did not preach isolation as a means to salvation but advocated living in the community and doing good.

The city of Lahore was once the chief city of a large area of northern India called the Punjab (the land of the five rivers). It was in the Punjab that Sikhism was born. Lahore is now part of Pakistan.

The Bowl of Milk and the Jasmine Flower

This is another story taken from the 'Janam Sakhis'. Guru Nanak preached his message of love and tolerance by giving simple practical examples, often in the form of hymns, accompanied by his Muslim companion, Mardana.

The Jealous Brother

The Sikh tradition behind this story is that Guru Ram Das sent his youngest son, Arjan, to Lahore to attend a marriage on his behalf. He gave him no instructions when to return, so the son obediently remained in that city. After a while he thought he would give the Guru a hint that he wished to return home. Prithia felt that he could advance his own cause in Arjan's absence and failed to pass on the letters from Arjan which were given to him to hand to his father.

The third part of the poem, not given in the story, reads:

'I am devoted utterly to the honoured Guru.

If I had not met you I should still be in darkness. When shall I meet you again, my Lord, the giver of good fortune?'

The point of the story is that the poem is not regarded by Sikhs as a human composition. It is divinely inspired, the word of God. For this reason Prithia was tongue-tied. He has not the power to utter this word. His brother, chosen by God to be the Guru, the spiritual teacher, has already been invested with this ability, though his father is still alive. Interestingly, throughout this composition Arjan never uses the word 'Father'. The human relationship is transcended by that of Guru and disciple, one which Prithia failed to attain.

The hymn occurs in pages 96 and 97 of the Guru Granth Sahib.

The Princes and the Guru's Cloak

Guru Har Gobind (1595–1645 CE), the sixth Sikh Guru, enjoyed an ambivalent relationship with the Mogul authorities. Sometimes he accompanied the Emperor Jahangir on hunting expeditions, at others courtiers played on the ruler's suspicions and he suffered his displeasure. On one such occasion the Guru was sent to the fortress at Gwalior and held there as a prisoner for over two years. When the Emperor realized that his official, Chandu, was jealous of the Guru and had tried to trick the Emperor, he ordered the Guru's release. However, the Guru realized that some Hindu rajas were also victims of injustice and decided to act on their behalf. The story tells how he succeeded in doing it.

A shrine at Gwalior commemorates the event.

The Merchant and the Five Hundred Gold Coins

Guru Har Krishan, before he died, said that his successor would be found in Bakala village. The Sikh movement was quite large by now and devotees gave considerable amounts of money to the Gurus who used it for the welfare of poor and needy members of society, not only Sikhs but Hindus and Muslims as well. Many men wanted to get their hands on these donations to use them for their own needs and claimed to be the 'Baba Bakale', the Guru living in Bakala to whom the eighth Guru had referred. This story shows how the true Guru, Tegh Bahadur, a man who served the community and defended the cause of the oppressed, was selected for his efforts. He was imprisoned and sentenced to death unless he denounced his beliefs and became a Muslim. His martyrdom is remembered each December.

The Story of Baisakhi

The Gurus ordered their followers to assemble in their presence twice a year at Diwali and Baisakhi, the spring harvest festival which is also new year according to one Indian calendar. In 1699 CE Guru Gobind Rai, as he was then called, was at Anandpur. The Sikhs came to him there in their thousands.

This story describes the important events of that assembly. Those Sikhs who received initiation became members of his new institution, the Khalsa, meaning 'the Pure'. Members of the Khalsa receive a special initiation, after which they must always keep the five 'Ks', so called because of their initial letter in Punjabi. They are:

    Kesh (uncut hair);
    Kanga (comb to keep it tidy);
    Kara (steel wrist band);
    Kirpan (sword);
    Kaccha (short trousers).

The Donkey and the Tiger Skin

This story explains one purpose of the Khalsa, to give the Sikhs a sense of identity, self-respect and pride which would enable them to be resolute in keeping the faith and defending the cause of the oppressed. The donkey, although he wore the tiger skin, did not behave like a tiger. Similarly, the Guru emphasized that Sikhs must be true to the uniform he had given them. Merely wearing the uniform was meaningless without noble actions.

The Water-carrier

Like Bhai Ghanaya who gave water to the Muslims, many Sikhs spend time helping others, wherever they come from and whoever they are. This service is called *sewa*. It generally involves work in the gurdwara that would usually be looked down on, like cleaning visitors' shoes or giving pilgrims water, or helping prepare food in the kitchen, known as *langar*. It may also include voluntary work in hospitals and day care centres.

The Sikh and the Buddhist

Tibet was conquered by the Mongols in the 13th century but Chinese authority weakened considerably over the centuries and had almost vanished by 1949. This enabled the Dalai Lama to exercise almost complete spiritual control as Tibet's Buddhist leader.

In 1951 the Chinese People's Liberation Army, realizing the importance of Tibet's position between China and India, invaded. By 1959 a revolt had broken out, during which the Dalai Lama fled to India. The Dalai Lama now lives in exile in a monastery at Dharamsala in India. He continues to travel and receive visitors.

The Padma Shri is an annual award given for distinguished achievements and usually awarded to citizens.